Another Place

MIKE BARLOW's first collection *Living on the Difference* won the Poetry Business Book and Pamphlet Competition 2003 and was shortlisted for the Jerwood Aldeburgh Prize for Best First Collection. He has won prizes in a number of competitions, including first prize in the National Poetry Competition 2006, the Ledbury Competition 2005 and the Amnesty International Competition 2002. He is also a visual artist, making drawings, paintings and assemblages of found materials. He lives near Lancaster.

Also by Mike Barlow

Living on the Difference (Smith/Doorstop, 2004)

Another Place

Mike Barlow

CAMBRIDGE

PUBLISHED BY SALT PUBLISHING
PO Box 937, Great Wilbraham, Cambridge CB21 5JX United Kingdom

All rights reserved

© Mike Barlow, 2007

The right of Mike Barlow to be identified as the
author of this work has been asserted by him in accordance
with Section 77 of the Copyright, Designs and Patents Act 1988.

This book is in copyright. Subject to statutory exception
and to provisions of relevant collective licensing agreements,
no reproduction of any part may take place without the written
permission of Salt Publishing.

First published 2007

Printed and bound in the United Kingdom by
Biddles Ltd, King's Lynn, Norfolk

Typeset in Swift 9.5 / 13

*This book is sold subject to the conditions that it shall not,
by way of trade or otherwise, be lent, re-sold, hired out,
or otherwise circulated without the publisher's prior consent
in any form of binding or cover other than that in which
it is published and without a similar condition including this
condition being imposed on the subsequent purchaser.*

ISBN 978 1 84471 397 4 paperback

Salt Publishing Ltd gratefully acknowledges
the financial assistance of Arts Council England

1 3 5 7 9 8 6 4 2

To J
who keeps me in the real world

Contents

Aubade	1
June Bug	2
The Illustrator	3
Two Poems after William Maxwell	4
Evening Wind	6
Another Place	7
Choosing the Moment	8
House of Winds	9
Butterfly	11
The Boat in My Brain	12
Someone Else	13
South Westerly	14
Decoy	16
The Ball	17
Likenesses	19
The Sparkle in the Arctic Sky	20
Quviannikumut	21
A Night Out	22
Egg-finder	23
Sometime in June	24
Split-seconds	25
Hot Pursuit	26
The Old Faith	27
Versions of Heaven	28
Listening To It	30
The Man She Lives With	31
Something Between Us	32
The Third Wife	33
The Seven Days of Unst	34

Inside the Light	35
Prima Donna	37
A Hunger	38
Transit of Venus	39
The Real Dr Who	41
Mapmakers	42
Journey for Two Voices	44
My Neighbour	46
Fireproof	47
Confabulate	48
Real Life	49
Lament Played on an Umbrella	50
Putting Your Finger On It	51
The Barbs in Wire	52
Unspecified Crimes	54
Learning Not to Read	55
Reilly	57
Frisking The Poem	58
Unattended	59
Exit	60
Nocturne	61

Acknowledgements

Acknowledgements are due to the editors of the following publications: *The Independent on Sunday, Iota, Other Poetry, Poetry Review, Poetry Nottingham, Seam, Smiths Knoll, Staple, The Poetry Paper, shadowtrain.com.*

'The Third Wife' was winner of the National Poetry Competition 2006.

Aubade

My head's a strange room. You're there alone.
The stove glows, quiet as a train of thought.
Round your shoulders a herring girl's shawl—
lichen, ribwort, colours of an island
I make you up from. Outside it's night
and a wild one, wind's castrato in the wires,
a shed door banging, someone coming
and going to check the roof's tied down,
harbour lights bouncing on the water
like salmon trying to leap the pen.

You're reading. It's a letter. I think from me,
though it's odd I should write when I'm here
beside you. Any minute now I'll open my eyes
to a room outside my head. I'll squint
at the finger of light between the curtains, get up
to the view I see every morning, city towers
glinting in the sun, the runescript of cranes,
the small green rug ten storeys down, the Number 23
ticking over at the lights, noiseless from up here,
and the miniature newsvendor sipping a hot drink.

It'll all be exactly the same though subtly different
from the way I'm imagining it now
as I wait for the right instant to move.
Your warm skin sticks to me, your hand
twitches with its own electric dreams. Perhaps
you've not quite finished the letter which
come to think of it is probably about
the difficulty of living in two worlds at once.

June Bug

It must have been drawn to the reading light.
I was with Captain Cook in Poverty Bay, a place
so fertile and well settled the Maori wouldn't yield
an inch to the diplomacy of small arms fire
or beads. As the first warrior fell I heard a thump
in the room like a cupboard shutting or a book
falling to the floor. When I finally gave up
on the Captain, his misgivings, his ill spirits
misnaming a land, and forsook *Endeavour*
for my own berth, something slight and hard
dropped from the dark to scrape my cheek.
On my outstretched arm a scarab the size
of a finger joint, like a brooch of beaten copper
with a green armoured face. Still seized
by the zeal of the ship's quota of draughtsmen
and philosophers, I knew I should draw it
or take a photograph at least. But it was late.
I put it out, closed the window. Sleep
carried me up a creek where tattooed warriors
pulled faces, inedible fruit dropped from the trees
and for the first but not the last time, home
was an idea so remote I doubted it was real.

The Illustrator

Upstairs in the family semi, the main bedroom
given over to his studio, you'd find the makings
of adventures months off yet: pen and ink roughs,
the gouache storyboard worked up image by image
until a horse, half chestnut half white page and ridden
by a pencilled ghost, cantered right towards
the next blank frame and cunningly suspended ending.

Cluttering the room the real things: leather chaps
like oblong sails, spurs, bridles, Stetsons.
On the mantelpiece a Derringer pistol once
slipped into an evening bag or stuck in a garter.
Handle first he offered me a Colt .45
my twelve-year-old arms could barely lift
without his hand propping up the barrel.

He cocked the hammer, spun the empty chamber,
explained the kick, how most fired wide or high:
in those days, if you were shot, chance was
it wasn't meant for you. He stroked a polished handle.
You'd be surprised. Complaints pour in
if toolwork's wrong on a Smith & Wesson
or I miss some detail on a saddle.

In the window bay, instead of a dressing-table
or Lloyd Loom chair, an easel held a painting
of a steamboat thrashing the Mississippi night.
From its lit windows I could hear a Dixie band,
the laughter of dangerous women
eyeing the gambler with his bootlace tie. On deck
silhouettes in stovepipe hats smoked cigars and stared
into the dark, trying to make us out across the water.

Two Poems after William Maxwell
('In desert country the air is never still.' The Folded Leaf)

    1

In the country where those who can't speak
and those with nothing to say choose to live,
an old man leads a moon-eyed mare.

He can tell a thunderstorm's coming by the wind
as it soughs round his earth-sod house.
There is much he can teach us.

But it's the children, the desert children,
we must listen for first, the sing-song
tricks of their games, their word for stranger.

You'll know when you hear it. It means cousin,
which means they'll share their bread, their fire,
the clothes on their back.

It's a word you'll hear them call out to dogs,
deer, geese, a word they'll honour you with
should you be lucky enough meet them.

2

In the pebbled river, in the wind
as it fingers rods of grass,
in the circumspect whisper of blown sand,
another life: the voice of an old woman perhaps,
or a man scything hay.

In the distance a windmill
swings its bone white arms. This
you don't hear. If we close our eyes
it won't be there.
Reality can never exist
through one sense alone.
Think of the strained faces of the deaf,
the inward look on a blind face.

The world suggests itself
continually and we respond, continually
making our way over mountain and desert
to tended lawns and raked ponds
where a gardener talks to himself in his sleep.

Evening Wind
after Edward Hopper

I'm passing through. Who knows
where to. Upriver, upstate. Wherever
there's skin, leaves or dust to unsettle.
But tonight it's New York. I billow
this curtain like a sail and there she is
up from the bed kneeling naked and surprised.
You may envy me the intimacy of her thighs,
firm stomach, those breasts you can't see
from where you are. I'm only the wind
but she knows otherwise. I goose-pimple flesh.

She goes to close the window. But doesn't.
Looks down there at the city, night lights
and traffic hum, the usual cliché, except
it's not a cliché, it's one of those moments:
life suddenly swung like a knocked gyroscope
and anything's possible. Nor does she
go back to bed. Instead she dresses,
gathers spare clothes, packs, picks up
cash and a pocket book, closes the door
quietly, takes the elevator to the street, hails a cab.
I bowl along wide-armed to greet her.

Another Place

They could have come by boat. You can see
there's a channel through the rocks.
They would have brought with them the timber they needed,
nails, corrugated sheets
and basic tools: saw, hammer, pick, spade.
They would have put up the roof by the first night,
first shelter, first title. There might have been rain
driving in from the west, or it may have been warm and clear,
like today, making everything feel right.
Later, the hearth, its stone trimmed and hefted into place,
some mortar, infill and the chimney
grown by muscle and eye into the main prop,
the one part that would last, a monument
to forgotten labour on an empty coast.
Early on they would have planted the rowan,
perhaps a whip brought from another place, and the holly,
to ward off evil. And here are roses
gone wild among the rusty iron and rotting creels.
Tall blue flowers that don't belong in these parts
are signs of a garden where cattle now wander and browse,
leaving the poisonous flowers which,
like the old iron bedstead propped inside,
still anchor the place to a history.
Otherwise, there are no ghosts here, only us,
dreamers from away, picking about, reading signs.
Us and our conjectures.

Choosing the Moment

I'll choose my moment: sea fog, no sign
of the cockle-gatherer, his old blue van.
I'll come up on the blind side, slip through
the doorless doorway, light a fire.

It'll need new lights seaward, a couple of panes
at the back. I'll work quietly at first, straining
to catch boots on the track or a car door slam.
Clear days I'll keep an eye on the horizon.

If no one comes possession will settle in me:
the door rehung, slipped shingles fixed,
stack and ridge repointed, traps set,
holes in the skirting plugged.

In the roofspace there could be letters, a bible,
a shepherds manual, cuttings from the life of Elvis.
Each morning a one-legged gull
will tap the window till I give it crusts.

Back end she says she'll join me.
I'll wait out lengthening nights, first snow
passing to fall inland. Lamplight will cast
the room's reflections through the dark.

I'll look out at myself and there she'll be,
a smile that might be a blemish in the glass.
Imagine her reaching to touch me, both of us
afraid we'll move at the wrong moment.

House of Winds

NORTH

No doors face that way.
We keep watch through a squinch.

An army's barked orders, whistled signals,
the creak of cumbersome wheels.

All leave cancelled, letters home
censored. There's no outfacing the ice-
queen's smile, her armoury of splinters.

EAST

A winter blade through
bone-thin gaps and cracks,
angling for flesh. A stoat
scuttles in the roofspace,
the washing line whines.

In summer it's a Baltic kiss,
goosefeather cool, carrying
the scent of heather from the hills,
scorching the leaves of roses.

SOUTH

The warm breath of amnesia,
promises made and never kept. Prodigal
brushing aside the skirts of curtains
to return glad-handed, scatter
pink sand from the Sahara, cargos
of exotic bugs. A strange bird
blown off course scouts the garden,
unwitting herald from another parallel.

WEST

Cockle breath, the tail end
of hurricanes, Caribbean spun.
Waves of rain against the gable end,
snapped ash, jug-band music in the flue.
Waltz or jig we dance its temperate dance,
plant by it, harvest, lean into it
like old salts unsteady on the land, listening.
It speaks in tongues, its narrative
a prophesy we turn a deaf ear to.

Butterfly

An ocean bursts against cliffs, dislodges a handful of shale
and a fossil. Five storeys up a man with a hammer
demolishes the wall he stands on.
A crofter lifts potatoes in the rain. A long way east
a foghorn barges into the yachtsman's dream.

One sleeping body curls round another
whose cells cluster and multiply.
A swallow flies into a window and lies stunned.
Lights and dancing in the High Street
celebrate a deft cross in extra time.

Mars winks red and a rocket lands in a lemon grove.
On the radio a politician answers her own questions,
not ours, nor those keeping a child awake
as he listens to his parents downstairs. If it rains
where you are, in another hemisphere the land will bake.

When you feel the wind change
think of icebergs calving, the political climate
moving towards its opposite, the pollen count falling,
the Dow Jones closing up, a mirage
luring a lost tribe as it searches for the sea.

The Boat in My Brain

has long since slipped its moorings, cast off
from the quayside, the rower
jumped for dry land, away
to the nearest bar to lose himself.

The painter's spliced end trails the surface
like a finger on an idle afternoon,
rainwater sloshes across the boards
and a tin baler clinks its bell.

It bumps me in the night, breaks
the current of a dream, wakes me
as a turning tide
might nudge a dozing pilot. I jump.

My weight rocks the strakes
like old scales
suddenly struck into life. I bale,
slide oars through rowlocks and pull

with no clue where I'm heading,
whether back to the quay
where a lost figure waits
or out to the grinning horizon.

Someone Else

The two foot ledge cants me outwards.
To stay put I have to bend one leg,
brace against the heel; below,
the sheer grey wall, the dangle of rope,
pebble faces squinting from a skirt of scree.

I pay out, the red line inching upwards.
So scared I couldn't spit I swear
I'll take up golf or Scrabble,
long for office politics,
a lukewarm pint in a smoky bar.

A tug. *Climb when you're ready* plumb lines
through the gut, the heart flies round its cage.
Someone else, not me, draws a deep breath,
swings past a bulge of rock to seize
a pinch grip on the edge of all that air.

South Westerly

We crawled like insects, bodies as close
    to the shapes of the rock as possible.
I think back now and feel
    the unwieldiness of limbs,

how we shouted to one another
    just to hear, to know we were really there,
in the rush and howl, the sting of grit,
    those invisible punches.

And below us we could see
    the troubled eye of the tarn
whipped to a cloud of spray
    driven up the scree like rain.

Instinct told us we should turn round.
    But with our backs to it
we feared being lifted, tossed
    like bits of tumbling moss.

So we crawled on and it seemed
    to enter our bloodstream,
inflate us so we had to anchor fingers
    round the edges of rock

or grab makeshift ropes of cowering grass
    to stop ourselves taking off
like dirigibles, all the time leaning,
    inching forwards, grinning.

And grinning at what? It was more
        than the clenching of teeth,
the involuntary rictus of effort, more
        than wind moulding our soft masks.

I saw it in your eyes.
        You must have seen it in mine
because your grin
        widened when you looked my way.

Decoy

I'm a trailed wing in the meadow
crying *Here no here no here*
drawing you despite yourself
further and further from home.
Or closer to home, let's say
I'm paw marks on a freshly painted floor,
out into the street, round the corner
and away onto waste land
where toads and lizards colonize
old tyres and fridges.

Or I'm the wave reflected
in a shop window, gone
when you turn of course
but breaking thought for long enough
to throw you off the scent.
And I'm the News, The Shipping Forecast,
a bass beat boosted from a car window;
voices from the ginnel, the row
quiet neighbours have
when their children are away.

And I'm the mutter of the town at night
that keeps sleep shallow
or the silence of the country so complete
phantom noises chase you through the dark.
You run. I follow, closer
than you think I'd dare. I'm there
to catch your eye, your ear,
your nerveless heart,
until it stops.

The Ball

Slow down you said, look.
We were mid-island, as far
as you could get in any direction
from the sea, the intricate danger
of cliffs and stacks,
arches sunlight drank through,
drongs and dizzying geos;
or from voes of quietened water
gently rocking yachts and yoals
while the ocean beyond
struck land with a force
you could feel in your core.

Here there was nothing
but shoulders of moor,
a scudding sky and the road
twisting and rolling ahead and behind,
not a building, shack or shed
in any direction, that far from the coast
where a seabound folk's
timber houses wore
white-framed windows and looked
surprised at the view
across to the lighthouse
or down to the pier.

Here there was nothing
and here was a man bouncing a ball,
a tennis ball, along the road.
Bounce, catch. Toss, catch.
No break in his casual stroll.
Glasses skew-whiff, shirt hanging out,
he wore a slight smile as if
this was all you had to think about
when you walked from nowhere

to nowhere in the middle of nowhere,
this is what it meant
to be at the centre of things.

Likenesses

You're walking along a beach,
a steep slope of pebbles sliding under your weight,
the sound of a hundred voices
saying the same thing
but not in unison.

What you're looking out for
are small washed-up objects that remind you of others,
pieces of silvered wood like fish, a stone
like an eye, a rusty nail
like a used toothpick.

When you look up there's a stranger
coming your way. Something familiar makes you uneasy,
perhaps the mole on the left cheek or a hand
in a pocket jiggling change
the way you do.

The figure stoops, picks something up,
offers it. You feel its weight, its shape, notice the colours,
the patterns on its surface, how light strikes it.
You've no idea what it could be
or what it reminds you of.

But you have to speak. There's an urgency
about this stranger's look, a need to know, a need
for explanation. The face in front of you
is both very old and very young.
It won't take no for an answer.

The Sparkle in the Arctic Sky

is not the Northern Lights
but a firework show. There is
the promise of dancing
until dawn

and caribou, seal and walrus
and the south wind
which is a good wind
for walrus;

but we cannot only be
a part of the world we once had,
for it is hard to get anywhere now
without a skidoo

and on the radio
we are talking in our own language
but about our language too.

(source: Mike Donkin, *The Independent* 10 April 1999, on the Inuit achieving control of their land, Nunavut.)

Quviannikumut

Find it left on a bus or in a station bar
you won't know where to send it.
I never bother with the first page—
name, address, car number, next of kin.

But I keep the crucial numbers up to date:
tandoori takeaway, Chinese herbalist,
plumber, the woman who'll do for me
when the mess I live in's done for me.

ADDRESSES includes too many names
I can't put faces to now,
and the last five places
my daughter's lived this year.

FINANCIAL's blank. INFORMATION
carries a small map of Iceland,
the quickest bus between Wigan and Leigh,
and my fastest time up Clougha.

Without the DIARY I'd get by.
Anniversaries and outpatients
have a way of coming round again.
So do friends you owe a call.

It's under NOTES you'll find the vital stuff,
the finger spelling alphabet, hints
on calculating hyperfocal distance,
the formula for dating hedgerows.

So, thumb the pages, spare a thought
for a life deprived: no Naismith's Rule,
Fibonacci series, speed of sound,
no Inuit word for indescribable happiness.

A Night Out

What I'd like to do now is sit out in a deckchair
under the old oak by the vegetable patch,
jigsaws of evening light moving across me in the breeze.
I'd like to sip a chilled stout and beside me
have a book I know I'll not read. I'd like you
to bring supper on a tray—broad beans, potatoes
and salad please, followed by ripe peaches
whose juice we'll taste on each other when we part.
I'll stay there as the darkness grows out of the ground,
thickening the silhouettes of trees, fall asleep
among the cricks and rustles and well past midnight
wake to the smell of damp grass and a dew on my beard.
When first light's turned to sunrise I'll come indoors,
clamber in carefully beside you like an old dog fox
with nothing to show for the night but himself.

Egg-finder

She found the first signs in the hedge along the top field,
crow-pecked scoops of shell scattered like shrapnel.
Then one whole, an elliptical planet soft-landed in dead grass.
This she pocketed, took back to the house, examined
numbered and dated. She opened the ledger
and in her meticulous hand described where she found it,
its scuffs and blemishes, particularities of shape.
Two days on she found the second, a beckoning dewstone.

There were nine all told, each appearing after a clear night,
as the moon waned from gibbous to pig to paring;
as if something of the stars' glimmer had coalesced
in boneblack shadows to lay a rimy crust
on pebbles from a Paleolithic sea. She placed them
in straw in an old box on top of the Rayburn,
turned each one daily until she judged it time enough
to try them on the cold floor, check for the tremors of life.

The night they hatched she was woken by the cries
of sea creatures suddenly given air to swim in.

Sometime in June

As if for some purpose the days
    get longer and longer.
        They'll go on like this until
there's no night and the moon
    leaves, gives up on its pallid
        daylight ghost to emigrate,

try its luck in the other hemisphere,
    dragging the tide behind it,
        leaving the boat we dream in
high and dry above low water mark,
    taking with it the light
        we touch each other by, the sound

of a violin tuned to the future tense,
    the stove's glowing silence,
        the knock of friends who drop by
on the off-chance, moments
    of insight, the transit of months,
        the astrologer's inspiration;

until one of us turns to the other
    and says, as if for some purpose,
        remember the nights how they
used to get longer and longer,
    how we feared where the silver
        light we now long for would lead us.

Split-seconds

The eloquence of a slammed back-gate.
The clunk of the exhaust
as you take the cattle-grid too fast
(how it makes you wince if I do that).
But still I put my head round
the door of your room to check
if you're online. The screensaver's glow
changes the colour of the walls,
your empty chair orbits Mars or Mercury,
skims the clouds of Jupiter, surfs
the rings of Saturn. I spin
in a capsule of soft changing light
while, crouched in corners, a crew of shadows
fiddles with controls no-one understands.

Any minute now I'll be weightless,
reach, slow-motion, for the table edge,
the ceiling light, the chair leg, anything
to bring me back to myself, give me a hold
I can wrestle the room to the ground with.
All this in the time it takes to remember
the gate bang, picture you out there,
one hand on the wheel, the other
changing up, lights in your eyes,
exhaust like a machine gun as the WPC
with the bulletproof vest makes that
split-second decision: pull you over
or let it go because she knows you.

Hot Pursuit

My favourite position is riding pillion.
There's a mole on the back of your neck
I focus on as I put my arm round your waist,
knead your belly, press the hot
cobbles of your bum into my lap.

0–60 in 5.3 seconds,
north up the M6 on the outside lane,
wheelies round traffic cones,
bursting paper hoops, jumping rings of fire,
the sleep police in hot pursuit
for unlicensed use of a certain dream.

We reach road-end at Duncansby Head
where you give the throttle a final twitch
and take off on a long ascending arc,
the bike falling from us to the sea
as we glide like Chagall lovers
down the chute of the Northern Lights.

As usual it's a soft landing
when we wake and roll apart.
You're having a hot sweat.
I'm bursting for a pee.

The Old Faith

Before they put a convex mirror
like Cyclops' eye on the blind
T-junction by The Punch Bowl,
you used to have to cross
your fingers, hold your
breath and pray. From the left
you risked young farmers
hitting the hump bridge like
a take-off ramp. And from the right
a builder's flat-out wagon rattling
loose planks and scaffolding
might aim itself between
the gable ends. It was no
black spot though, policed
we suspected, by its own
assiduous deity, able to bestow
last minute caution or second sight.

Now he's redundant we wonder how
he occupies himself. There's talk
at closing time of long meanders home
stalked by a presence not quite visible,
how turning suddenly you'll see
a thorn bush freeze in moonlight,
or hear a farm dog's bark
split darkness down the middle.
A stranger in old overalls prompts nods
and nudges in the bar. Meanwhile
technology's all-seeing eye
grows cataracts of frost, glares
in the sun, weeps grime and slush
so we're none the wiser, dither still,
and lurch, the heart misfiring,
as we mutter prayers we fear
there's no one left to listen to.

Versions of Heaven

MODERN
(after The Weather Project, Tate Modern)

In the Turbine Hall a steaming sun's trapped
low on the horizon, forever dawn and promising
too much. Two hundred feet above us
a ceiling of mirrors makes constellations of our bodies
sprawled on the floor below. I find myself
by looking for the Chinese student ten yards to my left.
With her red bomber jacket she could be Mars.
I'm darker, the odd glint from my glasses
a reflection light years from its source. Remembering
my semaphore I send a message, but the mirrored letters
spell a name I've never come across before.

PERPENDICULAR
(Peterborough Cathedral)

One hundred and forty feet above the congregation
he's looking at you from the roof boss.
Bend your neck until the world begins to somersault
or lie prone on the flags and you might make out
the gold beard, fashionably forked for its time,
or perhaps the shining orb the left hand holds; but not,
from that distance, the careful detail of the palm,
the Mounts of Venus and the Moon, life line, heart line;
nor the knuckles and nails, the creases on the fingers
—index and first—extended in blessing. This
was one of God's games, playing the guildsman
so he could carve his son in his own image,
coming down more than halfway to meet us.

Listening To It

Imagine us, walking across a glass plain,
    our reflections shafts of shadow
        plumbing an inverted sky.

A shout from you and the world
    rings back, the made-up words of its song.
        Voices surround us, grow close, grow

shapes—figure shapes, a choir
    pressing at us, harmony and descant
        peeling away our worldly skins.

A shout from me and a drone
    joins in, pipe music, a pitch
        beyond lament, making the sound

a thigh-bone flute might make
    blown through by a north east wind.
        I reach to touch your cheek.

You flinch. Your smile, your other-
    worldly smile makes this much clear:
        you know, you've always known

were we to touch we'd fuse, the molten
    stickiness of glass, even as we know it
        cooling to transparent brittleness.

The Man She Lives With

The man she lives with quits home for days on end,
comes back with his hair full of burrs,
dew in his breath, green stuff under his nails.

It's not the silence he brings with him,
not the damp earth smell nor the pull
in the air as he passes. It's not the questions

she chooses to swallow nor is it the way he smiles
as if he's woken beside her after a good night's sleep.
Nor is it the feel of him, rougher than before.

It's a change of pressure in her head, like air cleared
by thunder, lightning's after-image, a zigzag
messenger coming her way but never arriving.

∼

The woman he lives with is telling a story. She offers him
a script to follow. The words in her eyes swarm
from their hive, hover and buzz round his head.

It's not the sense he can't make, the consonants
he chews to a grunt. It's not the masks she puts on
and takes off as the story grows, nor is it that look askance,

arched brow, grin begging a laugh, no questions asked.
It's not the way she moves the furniture in her sleep
so they wake up each day in a stranger's house.

It's what's hidden in the well of his brain, something
he can't reach, a silver toad perhaps that sings like Caruso,
the inside-out ornament of song.

Something Between Us

It goes back to the night we left the front door
wide open, woke to a breeze
breezing through like a bailiff,
a vagrant sunlight poking away at the corners.

It was nothing we could see or explain. It was
small acts of faith—a touch, a look—
suddenly misplaced. It was the way
one of us wasn't there when the other spoke.

It came to a head the night I got out of the bath
to be met by a toad at the bedroom door.
I blocked its escape with a book—
your favourite poet. Naked and superstitious

I shouted for help. Your laugh as you cupped
the visitor in your hands sounded
somehow complicit. On the doorstep
we watched it metabolising damp evening air.

By the time we realised it wasn't each other
we should have kissed but the toad, it was gone.

The Third Wife

My first wife knew no more than me, no telling
where her needs ended, mine began. One day though
I turned the hill to find the boat moored in the field,
the house out in the bay, adrift, door open wide.
I rowed out to a message on the mat: gone
to my cousin's place in Valparaiso

My second wife blew ashore in a force ten
leading a shipload of apprentices astray
with her white dress, her turned-up Nordic nose,
her precious bible clutched in a manicured hand.
No matter how I pumped, the organ of her heart played flat,
her painted smile as wooden as a figurehead's.

My third wife won't say where she lives.
She comes to me when the tides are right,
stays longer if a wind's got up or fog's come down.
I stroke the warm loaves of her biceps, kiss
dimpled elbows, listen for the souch
our breathing makes when we're together.

She has cousins everywhere. They post her money
in denominations the local shop won't take
or drop by uninvited while we're having tea. They push me
into corners, whisper her address. I turn a deaf ear.
This is my third wife I explain, who's known
many husbands, some worse some better than me.

The Seven Days of Unst

Tail-enders we were, just off the ferry, in for a week of fog,
the island an upturned boat cruising north in its cloud,
its wake to the south a boil of tides.

The first day brought skeletons of beached whales, a sea boot,
a piece of cabin, a muscle of hawser knotted round itself
like a complicated thought.

The second day a bonxie, robbed of anything to give it scale,
assumed Jurassic dimensions, a marauding shape tearing
its shroud of mist to flatten us against the beach.

On day three we sheltered in The Heritage Centre, scribbled
dialect words in note books, read up on the small print
of a hard life, a history of storm and shipwreck.

Day four we told the time by the caaing of sheep, the tap
of the wall-builder's hammer. At night the sky flashed
blue and green; we drew back from the windows.

On the fifth day we climbed to the island's keel but saw nothing.
The swell gave us sea-legs. Anglers after mackerel
cast lines down to an invisible bow wave.

On the sixth day the fog lifted and there it was, the horizon's
perfect circle, us its unmapped centre, a hazard
to shipping, a hazard to the known world.

By the seventh day we'd lost our language. The wind pressed
new words into our mouths. They tumbled about like tongues:
humliband, kabe, waarbie, shoormil, skroo, laebrack.

Inside the Light
(after Disappearance at Sea, by Tacita Dean)

The lighthouse sleeps in the last of the day,
its glass brain sea-washed mauve,

green, purple, grey and an amber spillage
across the convex ridges of the unlit lens.

Like an inquisitor peering into an eye
for signs of the true faith all you find

are clear buds of unlit glass, their coiled
filaments the thoughts a hundred thousand

candles wait to think, and a mirror giving back
what you know is there already,

sea-washed grey, green, purple, mauve
and that amber spillage, and now and again

a tiny flash like a sudden wave halfway out
or the streak of a whale or a sail dipping forever.

Below, or above, or somewhere within
comes the banging machinery of voices

a belly sound about the business
of setting things right, a conversation of echoes,

no words but a gravity of tone like the final
blessing a drowning man might listen for.

~

Dark's scheduled moment drops and the beam
sweeps candlepower into your skull,

a probe whose bright ellipses scrape
a cliff the psyche clings to like a climber

cut off by the sea and no way up,
a figure or the likeness of a figure

picked out from lichen and the fissures
water, salt and wind have drawn in rock.

And the screech of sea-birds or a brewing gale
like tinnitus reaches its crescendo to reveal

the word of god as an ordinary word
signifying anything you want.

And then, look—not quite swallowed
by the fathomless night, pale movement,

a shadow of light defining itself as it tacks
to the right and hits, each time round

the same bit of sea where something
we can't explain is always happening.

Prima Donna

Shelves gleam with jars: crystals,
phosphorus, rare insects and mammoth hair,
a sea anemone (for its sensitivity)
and one of Einstein's eyes,
its clear intelligent blue
piercing him wherever he turns.

This morning though it's sand,
the singing sand he pours into a flask.
Thumb and forefinger on the neck,
he holds it to the light.
With the first shake
a faint rasp hovers in his ear.
He tunes the amplifier, shakes again.
This time he thinks he hears the sirens whisper.
Another shake and chimes
from the sea's depth ring for him.
Eyes closed now and ears alight
he grasps the neck, swings it like a handbell.
A clear soprano wavers, gathers
before its spear of sound smashes the glass
to burst fortissimo into the room.

To the air's applause
jar upon jar cracks.
Formaldehyde and brine swim together.
The stick of phosphorus ignites.
The sea anemone cries.
And that eye stares up at him, startled,
its blue already fading.

A Hunger

It's as if some truth's been missed, hidden
in particles of gabbro or the black plug of basalt;
or there's a thought I can't find, an absence
like deer beyond the next hill,
tracks in the peat the only clue.

It leaves me hungry, eager to dig down,
bury my face in soil, rub grit in my brain
till it bleeds insight. Old penitents
would flog themselves, the sugars
in the blood inducing trance.
I want to come back from a new idea
changed, the balance tipped
and equilibrium found again but this time
with a slight quiver as if some
aftershock still rumbled on,
as if there were no time left and it didn't matter.

The sea moves, rock weathers, flowers —
tormentil, orchid, eyebright —
shake in the wind whether or not we name them.

Transit of Venus

So, good Captain, you had your orders.
Tahiti. A ship of pressed men perhaps
seized from a homebound merchantman;
or landsick tars the streets of Wapping
threw out in the small hours;
midshipmen sons of gentlemen
reciting bad poetry on windless days;
draughtsmen, artists, an astronomer, a botanist.
And sealed instructions to be opened after the event.

Your observatory, a shrine to science,
erected on a point of land pulled up
from the sea-bed by a crab-god
fishing for a midday snack.
You watched through a hazy sky
but in the end the vital measurements
eluded everyone, the world not ready yet
to give us a proper fix on our position.

I missed it too, Sir, 235 years later,
the chance of a lifetime and the heavens shy.
At Greenwich though, they were queuing up
for telescopes and dark glasses,
lenses over white sheets where the evening star
revealed its daytime self as a neat bite
bored by a light-eating insect.
Up here cloud had us mundane and sweating,
mending fences, keeping accounts.

Alright for you. You had that seal to break,
fresh orders (as if you hadn't guessed already
the quest for the southern continent).
Man of your time, Captain, you took your business

where you had no business, brought goodwill,
gunfire and disease, gave strange worlds a bearing
on each other. For us, now, the Atlas is complete,
digital, the globe web-cammed, our only sealed papers
poked in a drawer for those we leave behind.

The Real Dr Who

He'll appear at some moment in between:
you'll be pouring last night's soup down the drain
or plucking goose-grass burrs from your jacket.
Or the last bus home will stop where there's no stop
for a stooped stranger escaping the rain,
jiggling tomorrow's change in his pocket.

You'll know him by smell: a struck match gone out,
sweat of bronze, or the whiff of copper circuits,
that too-clean tang from sheets dried in fresh air.
He may expect you to guess, read his mind.
He may not want to talk. He's seen too much
or too little. Nod, let him know you're there.

Think stars going out, light years imploding,
desert oblivions, no torch beam glint
from eyes, single, double or multiple.
No wonder he wants to touch you, feel time
stand still. When he tugs your sleeve, pats the back
of your held-back hand, you'll feel it as well.

Mapmakers

The British sent Nain Singh to map the route
    to Lhasa, incognito through forbidden land.
Had he been caught he would have lost
    his head, this unassuming merchant
faking his devotions with holy beads,
    prayer wheel and hidden sextant.

Today, such spies are blatant, measurers,
    mapmakers everywhere. They live
among us like ordinary men and women,
    figures invisible in day-glo,
wielding theodolites along suburban avenues;

knobbly-knuckled dowsers, modest meter readers,
    bank clerks, tellers of minutiae;
statisticians dreaming the perfect fit, data
    to die for; stargazers, their imaginations
dwarfed inside enormous instruments.

But under cover still, the undetected traveller
    slips repeatedly across the border
from the left brain to the right, measured paces
    tallied on his rosary, a twirling
prayer wheel packed with calculations

by which he seeks to straighten out the soul's
    clandestine muddle; beware, he'll pull
the loose threads from the coat of ritual,
    reveal you to yourself as no more than the sum
of small integers, carried over and forgotten,

much like Nain Singh himself, for all his
    painstaking sums and sightings, the subterfuge,
the loyalty. No price an empire won't demand:
    a life being other than you are, as if to fix
the altitude of a many-windowed palace
    could reveal the many faces of its god.

Journey for Two Voices

When you board the train look for a seat
facing the engine and next to the aisle
so you can make an easy exit.

It's always a matter of having
somewhere else to go

Wait half an hour then visit the toilet,
change the colour of your eyes with tinted lenses,
stick tattoos on your hands.

somewhere nothing's what it looks like

If anyone tries casual conversation
avoid eye contact and smile.
Innocent questions are a giveaway.

and language an illusion of wisdom.

When you reach your first scheduled change
sit tight. Five minutes later the train will stop
at a deserted halt where a weathered sign reads
DO NOT ALIGHT HERE.

Stopping places, swapping places
places on the edge

This is where you get off.
At the end of the platform, walk down the ramp
where willowherb and bramble choke the sidings.

a day's walk from here to there

Climb the fence to reach a road
leading to a small town where everyone
will be wearing mirror shades.

where the reply you get when you ask the way
is a version of the truth, misunderstood.

Find the post office, send a postcard
to your last address. Outside I'll be waiting.
You'll know me when you look for my eyes
and see your own face peering back.

My Neighbour

heard voices through our party wall.
They jeered, whispered, gossiped,
    laughed all night at jokes he didn't get,
tapped messages in prison Morse
    down air-locked pipes.

Like a squaddie on a house search,
he shouldered in the backdoor,
    rushed the place in broad daylight
psyched-up and jumpy as a ghost
    haunted by the memory of its shadow.

He left behind flung-open cupboards,
yawning wardrobes, his spoor
    from the street, splintered glass
trodden into lino and a piece
    of his mind which hung in the air
for weeks, its spittle and obscenity.

Now, when I talk to myself
I choose my words with care,
    in bad light look away from mirrors
where a stranger might be staring back.
    At night I bolt both doors,
press my ear against the party wall.

Fireproof

The noticeboard's a curling skirt of circulars,
in-jokes and photographs of trawlers.
The floor's invisible beneath a pavement
of unfiled files. The weeping fig
weeps a sticky film over the radiator.

It's afternoon, midsummer, a time
and temperature you could snooze in were it not
for the figure in the other chair,
an old-fashioned skinhead spinning you a line,
his rank dog dozing by his side.

What you long for's ingenuity, an original way
to lose a giro or a reason for carrying a screwdriver
and hacksaw blade in enclosed premises
that bears believing. Your questions
are as see-through as his answers.

The fire bell goes. You've heard that before too.
He's away with his dog. You stay put.
This time the safety officer bursts in.
It's the real thing. At the assembly point
he has to take the count a second time.

When the sums are done you wander over
and peer back through your office window.
Smoke inside everywhere. Everywhere that is
except for an empty space the shape your body makes
when you try to look as if you're listening.

Confabulate

It's the gaps that matter.
Wiring the blanks with real life
as if real life were there still
not a sky deep hole
nobody can see you through.

Make sure both ends meet
in the middle, set off
from somewhere the present
makes believable. Cover your tracks
with the fiction of hard facts.

What you don't know only you
need know. What they don't know
they don't need to know.
It's a fine judgement
how little to admit to.

Living apart from yourself
is a trapeze artist's art, the safety net
an illusion. Miss the bar
and you'll fall through your own
blank space, instantly forgotten.

Real Life

It starts with the garden. One year
I leave the lawn to hay. Chickweed
reclaims the beds, meadowsweet
smothering the aquilegias. Next year
thistles, willowherb, jack-in-the-hedge.
Neighbours complain, look blank,
blind to the bog iris showing its tongues
or evening sun among the grasses.

What's indoors goes to Oxfam, car boots, the tip:
fridge, telly, the Bang & Olufsen,
books—a sea of words
I nearly drowned in once—shells
from Corfu, pebbles from Rascarrel,
dark glinting obsidian from Iceland.
Bare boards bounce to my tread, the house
light as a hot-air balloon tugging its mooring.

The day I leave I've only what I'm wearing,
the bagless traveller. I'm off to look for rooms
in Scalloway or Scarborough,
an abandoned suitcase gathering dust
in a wardrobe, or under a bed somewhere:
clothes in colours I never wear,
a dog-eared novel, the return half of a ticket,
a life I've not led waiting to lead me home.

Lament Played on an Umbrella

It was the eyes. Tell me about it, they invited. So I told her a dream: I was on Windermere, rowing. A stranger who looked like Stan Laurel sat in the stern. It was raining so he opened an umbrella and played a tune that made him cry.

The eyes narrowed as if she were watching a TV screen in the back of my head. Afraid subliminal messages might jump from my psyche, I switched channels, spun her a yarn about a country where you're not allowed to speak your own language and learning a new one changes your past.

Suddenly the number of the officer who knocked at the door flashed through my brain; he didn't know where to put himself or what to say. She nodded to let me know she too could tell when someone was holding back. The only people you can trust, I went on, are like my cousin who doesn't care what day it is so long as he's digging land-drains or taking an engine to pieces.

Ah. I can see your eyes glaze over. Hers did too. Don't fool yourself. You'd make no more sense than me, though I'm on familiar ground, a lifetime being heard and not heard at the same time. When they called the roll at school, I used to answer 'absent' but they put a tick against me all the same.

Putting Your Finger On It

Like the syntax of an unfamiliar language,
like a torch killing night vision,
like a rabbit's foot charm
gone from its place on the mantelpiece.

Like the front door left open all night,
the phone off the hook
and still ringing, like a story
that only falls open on prime numbered pages.

Like a jigsaw puzzle of endless sky, the last word
on silence, like the shortest distance
between two moving points, a street map
of Liverpool for planning a walk in the Lakes.

Like next week's weather, like a memory
locked in the glove compartment,
a holiday video on rewind,
an insight into the mind of an early life form.

Like a pub quiz with no questions, last orders
at opening time. Like a brain scan
in a thunderstorm, the calculus of dreams.
Like knowing all the answers and not having a clue.

The Barbs in Wire

And if the idea of it
gives you a buzz
            the sheer
circuitry, the crackle
of nervepods,
            the proprioceptors'
tipsy moment

remember the scream you woke from
one summer dawn
            distant cloud
stained red as juice
            or remember
coming in from the night
cold clung like a second skin

and the words of the prophet
and the interpreter's dream
and the sergeant's postcard home
            which read
all is going according to plan
            which is
according to plan.

So plant your boots
in the rose bed
            leave
your sack of feelings
wriggling by the backdoor
            or you'll come to

like a poacher in a tackle shop
keepnets and cartridges
spinners and flies
leathermen and dollies
            but no
clever gadget
for getting the barbs out of wire.

Unspecified Crimes

I knew him immediately from the way he looked
just like everyone else, from the way his eyes
stared somewhere beyond me, from the way a brief
anaesthesia came over me as I passed him.

It was rush hour. I turned. He was easy to follow,
not hurrying or dawdling. A man who knew
his place in the day, in his briefcase an empty lunchbox,
a holiday brochure, a few unfinished accounts.

Outside the tube he stood for a smoke, long drags
as if it were fresh air. A tug at cuff-linked cuffs, fingers
adjusting the knot of his tie like a pre-arranged sign
and he slipped underground. The Circle line, anti-clockwise,

to emerge ten stops later, take a maze of rights and lefts
like a man with a ball of string for a brain and a home
in one of those discreet Victorian squares built round
a small park of overgrown buddleia and balding grass.

When his key clicked I lost heart. I suddenly knew the rest:
a teenage daughter he was endlessly patient with; his wife
a lawyer or banker; his turn to cook, a bottle chilling, music,
Monteverdi say, or glam rock from his daughter's room.

He'd sleep the sleep of the impervious. Break in, stand
at the end of his bed to proclaim a litany of the world's
nameless and he'd dream on; press a lit cigarette
to his instep and he wouldn't as much as twitch.

I could shake his wife awake but she'd not hear me out.
Before she called the police I'd take the option of leaving.
As she showed me the door I'd tell her not to worry,
in the morning it would be as if I'd never existed.

Learning Not to Read
(after Italo Calvino, 'If On A Winter's Night A Stranger')

The trick is not to try too hard.
Once you close your eyes
or turn your head from the open page
you're lost, like trying not to think.

All those early struggles —
toilet training, tantrums, phonetics,
three letter words, then four,
bead strings of syllables —
they work their chemistry:

the polymer of grammar, chains of sense
binding us to continence and literacy.
We think we have no choice,
our syntax undegradable,
impervious to will.

But the trick is: keep on reading,
read everything you can, absorb
the very molecules of words,
allow the surds and sibilants,
fricatives and vowels

to play with you, inhale them
through the open valves of books,
their music, like a mantra,
stripping meaning down
to bones of sound.

At first a line or two will go,
or a sentence lift itself away,
then a paragraph, a page.
Eventually whole chapters
will be bleached clean,

the printed words evaporate,
language repossessed by roots,
a laugh, a shout, a croon,
simple noises no one can dispute.

Reilly

... and my name is Kelly, Michael Kelly
But I'm living the life of Reilly just the same.
                    MUSIC HALL SONG, 1919.

First thoughts are gravy and chips,
ice-cream in chocolate sauce and a cheese
so strong the brain sweats. Or it's
an open air jacuzzi on a balmy night,
an indigo sea and stars, scent on the breeze,
say cinnamon or cloves, and a long drink
with bits in it brought by a lover
half your age. It's a featherbed
and goosedown duvet, the blizzard outside
improvising scales on ancient instruments.

No hormone lapse, no loss of memory
or grip. Acts of God are double-edged:
struck down by a virus, you cancel plans
for a fortnight in the sun and miss an earthquake.
Charmed, the karma of a saint some say
or a cue for demons in the next life.
But when you've gone, be sure of this:
they'll talk about you in the present tense,
those hapless Kellys, the words
of an old-time song still echoing in their heads.

Frisking The Poem

Tucked under the collar is its pedigree,
illustrious names stretching back
through obscurity. Under the armpits
you'll find ideas incubating like eggs,
a revolver with five blanks and one live round
in case a shot of adrenalin's required.
In each side pocket are adjectives
disguised as penknives, adverbs
masquerading as keys. In the back pocket
the loose change of articles, definite and indefinite,
waiting to be taken out and put back again.
Inside the thighs a piece of plastic explosive
to show it means to be taken seriously.
Strapped to each ankle are wings.

Unattended

On the grass by the quayside, by the silted unnavigable river.
Where everyone walks to town and back all day, or feeds the gulls
or peers expectantly downstream as if the tide still brings sails.

Abandoned. Brown imitation leather, an oily stain on the lid,
locks shot, rough twine keeping slack jaws shut, corners
scuffed concaves, like a creature with its ears cut off.

Last night saw its contents arranged on the grass: a tin clock
without a tick, several pairs of socks (though he wore
bare feet in his shoes) a pile of exercise books I like to think

contained his life story, a tattered novel, wads of newspaper,
a crimson baseball cap. All checked and re-packed,
precise as a puzzle whose solution guarantees sleep.

And what did he dream with his head on the lid. A ship at last?
This morning no sign, just his case, conspicuous, a case
for public alarm, a taped-off street, sandbags and screens.

It wasn't the flash, the deafening, the smoke, the river's shudder.
It was time stopped but still carried about like treasure,
it was how an autobiography can never account for its ending.

Exit

There's a house with one entrance on the street of habit.
As you pass, the door yawns in its draught.

Take a sideways glance: you'll see down a hallway
that ends with a mirrored shadow's

sideways glance back out, as if it knows about you,
something you haven't grasped,

as if one day you might stop and enter, let the strut
and stammer of the city, the constant

traffic of thought fall away like conversation everyone
but you has given up on, one side

of your brain still listening for that last minute courier,
the rev of his bike, his zipped-up

package of urgencies, the other side playing chancer,
tossing the day's coin over your shoulder.

Nocturne

You can leave me with it, this sinkful,
the stumps of cauliflower, garlic skins,
spud peel, the gungy matter
a kitchen accumulates. This,
at the end of the day, is how I like it.
I gather pots, scrape away leavings,
soap froth dripping from my wrists.
My thumbnail scratches at a hide
of burnt sauce on the bottom
of a non-stick pan. Dusk
makes the window a mirror. I stare
beyond myself into arteries of sycamore.

It's your style to leave things to drain,
mine to dry and put it all away,
a fiddle tune in my head, high notes
almost disappearing before they plunge
to the bottom of everything, knives
in the knife drawer, spoons snug in their tray,
plates on their shelves, and always something
misplaced, on purpose: scissors
with the spice jars, the masher
behind the milk-jug, deliberate faults
woven into the day's back end,
a guarantee it's been the genuine thing,
while the musician signs off
with an intricate flourish and outside
the last bus climbs the brow, its lit shape
trundling home with no one on board.